HEALTH CARE
JOURNALISM

INVESTIGATIVE JOURNALISM THAT INSPIRED CHANGE

DIANE DAKERS

Crabtree Publishing Company

www.crabtreebooks.com

Author: Diane Dakers

Series research and development:
Janine Deschenes and Reagan Miller

Editorial director: Kathy Middleton

Editor: Janine Deschenes

Proofreaders: Wendy Scavuzzo, Melissa Boyce

Design and photo research:
Katherine Berti

Print and production coordinator:
Katherine Berti

Images:

Getty Images: Joshua Lott: p. 37 (top)
healthjournalism.org
   Screen Shot 2018-07-05 at 12.30.54 PM: p. 20
Istockphoto: Joe Potato: front cover (bottom left)
khn.org: Screen Shot 2018-07-05 at 2.36.28 PM: p. 30
Shutterstock
   Drop of Light: p. 6
   Leah-Anne Thompson: p. 7 (bottom right)
   REDPIXEL.PL: p. 43 (center right)
   Thinglass: front cover (newspapers), p. 1 (bottom left)
Wikimedia: Centers for Medicare and Medicaid
   Services: p. 25 (logo)
www.pulitzer.org
   Screen Shot 2018-07-04 at 3.22.34 PM: p. 5
www.reuters.com
   Screen Shot 2018-07-06 at 11.34.47 AM: p. 40
www.wvgazettemail.com:
   Screen Shot 2018-07-05 at 11.05.19 AM:
   p. 14 (bottom right)
All other images by Shutterstock

Library and Archives Canada Cataloguing in Publication

Dakers, Diane, author
     Health care journalism / Diane Dakers.

(Investigative journalism that inspired change)
Includes bibliographical references and index.
Issued in print and electronic formats.
ISBN 978-0-7787-5350-6 (hardcover).--
ISBN 978-0-7787-5363-6 (softcover).--ISBN 978-1-4271-2197-4 (HTML)

     1. Journalism, Medical--Juvenile literature. 2. Journalism,
Medical--Case studies--Juvenile literature. 3. Medical care--Press
coverage--Juvenile literature. 4. Health in mass media--Juvenile
literature. I. Title.

PN4784.M4D35 2018   j070.4'4961   C2018-905445-X
                                    C2018-905446-8

Library of Congress Cataloging-in-Publication Data

Available at the Library of Congress

Crabtree Publishing Company

www.crabtreebooks.com   1-800-387-7650

Printed in the U.S.A./122018/CG20181005

**Published
in Canada
Crabtree Publishing**
616 Welland Ave.
St. Catharines, Ontario
L2M 5V6

**Published in the
United States
Crabtree Publishing**
PMB 59051
350 Fifth Avenue, 59th Floor
New York, New York 10118

**Published in the
United Kingdom
Crabtree Publishing**
Maritime House
Basin Road North, Hove
BN41 1WR

**Published
in Australia
Crabtree Publishing**
3 Charles Street
Coburg North
VIC 3058

CONTENTS

INVESTIGATING HEALTH

Investigative journalists are reporters who deeply examine a topic or issue. Many work to uncover and report on issues in health care, such as addiction.

If you have a headache or a toothache, you might take a **mild** painkiller at home. But for many people, mild painkillers are not enough to ease the pain they suffer. People who are injured or suffer from **chronic** pain might visit a doctor to get stronger pain pills.

While these stronger medications help some people, others have a potentially deadly reaction to them—**addiction**. And sometimes, other people or businesses take advantage of the people suffering from addiction.

Companies that make and supply painkillers make money by selling them to pharmacies. The more people who depend on the pills, the more money companies can make by supplying them. Sometimes, other people such as pharmacy owners make money from high numbers of painkiller users, too.

In 2016, Eric Eyre, an investigative journalist in southern West Virginia, discovered that three huge American **drug** companies were doing just that. In a six-year period, the companies sold millions of prescription painkillers to pharmacies in small, rural communities—far more than the region's residents should need. They earned billions of dollars from those sales.

During the same time period, the number of area residents addicted to the drugs also increased. They took more and more pills at increasing **doses**. Many died of **overdoses**.

Since 1917, the **Pulitzer Prize** has awarded achievements in American journalism, music, and literature.

> [Overdose deaths] are destroying communities. We [in West Virginia] have the highest overdose death rate in the nation. The top four counties in the nation for overdose death rates are all in West Virginia.

Eric Eyre, 2017

The **profits** rolled in for the drug companies, doctors, and pharmacies. Addicts swallowed more and more painkillers. Before long, southern West Virginia faced the highest **overdose death rate** in the nation.

When Eric first "stumbled into" this story, he knew he had to expose the corporate greed that was leading to so many deaths in his community. It took him three years to pull the story together. To do so, he researched information about painkillers, accessed secret documents, reviewed data, and interviewed people grieving the loss of relatives who had overdosed.

In December 2016, the small newspaper Eric worked for, the *Charleston Gazette-Mail*, published his project, entitled "Painkiller **Profiteers**."

It led to **reform** in the prescription painkiller business and made such an impact in the community—and across the country—that it earned the nation's highest award for journalism: the Pulitzer Prize.

It's not every day that small-town newspapers win such impressive national awards. It's more common that big media organizations win Pulitzers, because they can afford to have large groups of reporters dedicated to investigative projects. But Eric's work proved that investigative reporting isn't just about having a big budget. As Eric's **editor**, Rob Beyers, described, investigative reporting is about having the "right attitude" and "dedication" to the community and to journalism.

IN-DEPTH JOURNALISM

The job of any journalist is to find stories, dig up facts, and report information to the public. Investigative journalism takes this process a step further.

Daily news reporters typically pursue stories that come from outside **sources**. Police and fire departments, government offices, and local businesses, for example, are sources that give reporters ideas for news stories. The reporters follow up on information they obtain from these sources. They ask questions, conduct interviews, and gather facts. Then they publish the information in local newspapers, on TV and radio newscasts, and online.

Investigative reporters, on the other hand, usually come up with their own ideas. They're often about things nobody has ever investigated before. These ideas come from a variety of places. Eric Eyre, for example, found his prescription painkiller story unexpectedly. He discovered some information about a court case that didn't make sense to him. His **instinct**, as an experienced journalist, told him he needed to ask questions about this information.

Curiosity and an instinct to ask questions are almost always the starting points for investigative journalism projects. A reporter might overhear a conversation that grabs his or her interest. A story might stem from a tip or a private document shared by a member of the public. Sometimes, investigative journalists follow up on questions that arise as they read or research other news stories.

The United Nations is headquartered in New York City.

WHAT IS INVESTIGATIVE JOURNALISM?

The **United Nations** defines investigative journalism as "the unveiling of matters that are **concealed** either deliberately by someone in a position of power, or accidentally, behind a **chaotic** mass of facts and circumstances—and the analysis and exposure of all relevant facts to the public."

That means investigative journalists uncover hidden stories, research them, and report them to the public. These stories might be kept secret on purpose. Sometimes, though, the stories aren't deliberately hidden—they're just buried so deep in documents, data, and details, that nobody has dug them up yet.

DIFFERENT REPORTING

People and organizations define investigative journalism in different ways. However, most agree that it differs from conventional reporting, or daily news reporting, in a number of areas:

INVESTIGATIVE JOURNALISM

- Reporter is **proactive**, takes initiative to find original stories
- Projects are long-term, in-depth, and require research
- Reporter's goal is to question
- Stories expose issues surrounded in secrecy or silence
- Work often leads to social change

CONVENTIONAL JOURNALISM

- Reporter reacts to information provided by sources such as police, governments, or businesses
- Reporting is short-term, usually daily news
- Goal of reporter is to inform
- Stories present the facts of the world as described by others, without digging deeper

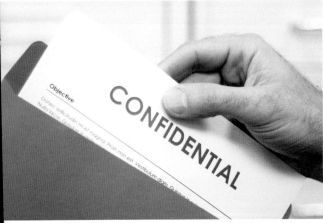

BREAKING NEWS Criticism Grows Over Trade Deal
LIVE NEWS ; in subway bombing • No agreement reached

*Investigative reporters often review stacks of documents, such as medical, **legal**, or government reports. This sort of research is **painstaking** and time-consuming.*

FINDING FACTS, PROVIDING PROOF

Once an investigative reporter has an idea, the research begins—and this takes time. While daily news reporters may produce a story in a day or two, investigative reporters typically need months, or even years, to pull together a solid report.

That's because, unlike news reporters who often have information from sources to begin with, investigative reporters start from scratch, doing research that's never been done before. It's also because they have to be absolutely certain that every fact and detail is correct.

All journalists check facts, but the investigative journalist always has much more information, data, and detail to **confirm**. They must check and double-check every piece of information before the story goes public.

Investigative journalists often produce stories that expose social concerns and wrongdoing by people in positions of power, such as the abuse of power or money. These types of stories might lead to changes in government **policies**, public outrage, or threats from people who don't want the stories told. Similar to a lawyer, an investigative reporter must prove all facts beyond a shadow of a doubt before publishing or broadcasting the story.

Because it can take many reporters and analysts many months to research and fact-check a piece of investigative journalism, it costs a lot of money. Many large newspapers have departments filled with reporters who focus on investigative journalism projects. A number of not-for-profit media foundations also do this type of work. Occasionally, small media organizations, like the one Eric Eyre works for, also manage to pull together projects that can spark nationwide change.

Other ways investigative journalists dig up details and verify information include interviewing sources, reviewing data, examining photographs and videotapes, and reading eyewitness reports.

HEALTH CARE JOURNALISM

Investigative journalists work to make a difference and right the wrongs in society. Their work may lead to change, but they are not **activists**. Activists are people who take action to push for change in specific areas. They might participate in protests, campaigns, and other activities designed to challenge governments and businesses. The job of a journalist, on the other hand, is to find the truth, not to promote a particular point of view or actively push for change.

Almost any topic can be the subject of an investigative journalism project—including the environment, sports, human rights, and in the case of this book, health care.

Health care journalists work to raise awareness and understanding of health and medical issues around the world. Their goal is to provide information, so members of the public can make informed, or well-researched, choices about health care. Health care journalists also seek to hold health care providers **accountable** for their decisions,

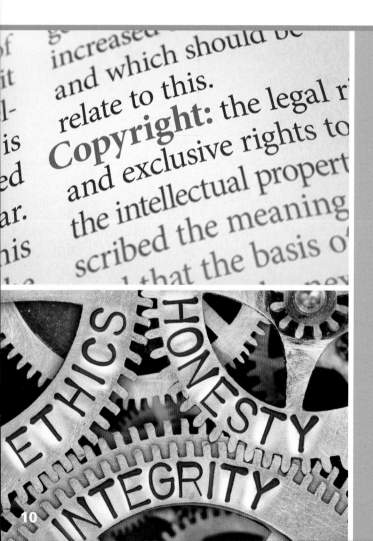

RULES AND ETHICS

As journalists conduct their investigations, they must follow certain laws. Many countries have rules about protecting the privacy of personal information, for example. There are also laws forbidding hate speech, which is language that attacks groups of people based on their race, gender, religion, or other identifiers. **Copyright** laws prevent journalists from using text, video, or audio without permission. There are also laws that prevent a journalist from **harassing** people to get information.

Journalists also follow codes of **ethics**. These are unofficial sets of principles, or guidelines, that outline acceptable and unacceptable behaviors. These include such things as commitments to **integrity**, fairness, truth, and accuracy.

the quality of their facilities, and the policies that affect citizens.

In recent years, investigative journalists around the world have covered such health and medical topics as abuse in nursing homes, **racial inequalities** in health care, the effects of loneliness on a person's well-being, and the continuing fight against diseases such as **malaria**, **polio**, and **HIV/AIDS**.

This book focuses on three specific health-related investigative journalism projects—a story about lead poisoning in children, a study of below-standard end-of-life care, and Eric's report on the companies that profited from other people's painkiller addictions.

The reporter on the lead poisoning story started with a question that came to him as he read another news article. The end-of-life care investigation began with a personal experience. And Eric's story, as you know, started when he stumbled upon some information that just didn't add up. All of these journalists had questions that needed answers.

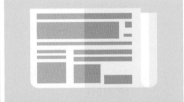

Multimedia presentations help investigative journalists to engage, or interest, readers; to present complex information in simple ways; and to reach wider audiences.

PRESENTING A PROJECT

Investigative journalism projects can be presented to the public in a variety of media. Media is the plural form of the word medium. A medium is a method of mass communication, a way to deliver information to a wide variety of people.

A newspaper is a medium that delivers printed stories, and radio delivers its messages by sound, while television broadcasts video images. The Internet uses digital technology.

Investigative journalism projects are presented through a variety of media. Today, many journalists are taking advantage of technology to produce multimedia presentations of their work. Such projects are usually presented online and can include photos, video, audio, and written components. Maps, charts, infographics, and interactive visual elements are also common.

"PAINKILLER PROFITEERS"

WHO	Drug companies, doctors, and pharmacies
WHAT	Contributed to high rate of overdose deaths
WHEN	2007–2012
WHERE	Southern West Virginia
WHY	For profit
HOW	To gain extra profit, oversold and over-prescribed painkillers to patients who became addicted; many addicts overdosed and died

Eric Eyre has worked for the *Charleston Gazette-Mail* for almost 20 years. His main job is to write stories about **politics** and issues that affect the state of West Virginia.

In 2013, while doing his regular work, Eric discovered some wrongdoing involving West Virginia's **Attorney General** and a number of **pharmaceutical**, or drug, companies. This led him to write many stories about the prescription drug industry over the next few years. He wrote about such things as the increasing abuse of illegal drugs in the region, government efforts to slow that abuse, and the legal battles faced by the Attorney General who was accused of wrongdoing.

Investigative journalism projects often evolve or spin off from other work. Eric's work on the drug industry led him to an even bigger story. He discovered that the state of West Virginia had filed a **lawsuit** against the drug companies involved in his original set of stories. Eric knew the lawsuit had something to do with prescription pain pills. Other than that, he knew nothing about it— but one detail struck him as odd. The documents related to the lawsuit were **sealed**. That meant they weren't available to the public, as most government documents are.

As a good investigative journalist, Eric's curiosity and instinct kicked in. He knew there must be something in those documents worth hiding. He sensed there was more to this story.

Because Eric has a full-time job as a daily news reporter, he wasn't able to drop everything and follow this new idea. In a 2017 interview, Eric explained that at the small newspaper where he worked, each reporter had to produce a "story or two a day" to keep the newspaper running. This made it difficult for any reporter to find time to complete large investigative projects. Still, Eric managed to "chip away" at his research after his other work was done for the day.

Alongside his regular work, Eric also wrote more stories about the prescription drug business. He exposed crooked doctors and **pharmacists** who supplied addictive painkillers to people who were hooked on them. These crooks also sold pills to other people who, in turn, sold them to addicts. Some of these doctors and pharmacists were, in effect, drug dealers.

Eric then focused his attention on the role of the drug companies. He wanted to investigate how they contributed to the problem. He suspected the secret was hidden in those sealed documents.

CLASSIFIED

Eric had a feeling the lawsuit documents had information that was being hidden for a reason.

A LOPSIDED BATTLE

Investigative journalists often face obstacles while trying to collect information and prove claims. Accessing documents that others would like to keep private is one common obstacle.

In the spring of 2016, Eric and his newspaper went to **court**. They asked a judge to unseal the documents related to the lawsuit. They argued that the public had a right to know what was in them.

The drug companies opposed the request. They hired lawyers to argue in court that the documents protected **trade secrets**. The drug companies also pointed out that they do nothing more than sell painkillers. They said the problem was with bad doctors and pharmacists who put the pills in addicts' hands.

While the drug companies had 30 highly paid lawyers on their side, just two small-town lawyers, who worked for free, represented the newspaper. This lopsided court battle was one of the biggest challenges for Eric in this investigative journalism project. "These companies are huge," he said in a 2017 interview. "They put up a tremendous fight to block us […]They tried to keep their drug sales data secret."

Still, after two months, masses of legal paperwork, and multiple court sessions, the judge agreed with the *Charleston Gazette-Mail*. He ordered the documents unsealed. The following day, Eric wrote an article about their contents.

The judge agreed with Eric and his team that, given the prescription drug overdose death rate in West Virginia, the public had a right to know what the drug companies were hiding in the sealed documents.

Charleston Gazette-Mail
A Pulitzer Prize-Winning Newspaper

NEWS   BUSINESS   OPINION   SPORTS   LIFE   A & E   OUTDOOR PURSUITS   BLOGS   OBITUARIES   DAILY MAIL

Unsealed court filing details drug firm's pain-pill shipments to WV

Eric Eyre   Nov 7, 2016   (0)

Henry Jernigan, a lawyer representing Cardinal Health, argues before Boone Circuit Judge William Thompson last week that records showing how many pain-relief pills the giant drug company shipped to specific pharmacies in West Virginia should remain secret.

REVEALING THE TRUTH

Eric wrote that the papers revealed that the state of West Virginia had sued a number of drug wholesalers for their role in West Virginia's "ongoing prescription drug problem." Wholesalers buy large quantities of drugs from manufacturers, store them, then sell and ship them to pharmacies around the country.

At the time, West Virginia had the highest drug overdose death rate in the country. Two types of strong prescription painkillers—hydrocodone and oxycodone—contributed to more deaths than any other drug.

The paperwork showed that wholesalers shipped massive quantities of those painkillers to small, community pharmacies between 2007 and 2012. The number of painkillers being supplied and sold was much more than any small town needed. One wholesaler, for example, shipped more than 300,000 tablets of hydrocodone to a town with a population of 808 people. "That amounts to 350 hydrocodone pills per person" in the town.

The lawsuit suggested that the wholesalers knew they were shipping too many pills. These pills are highly addictive, so the extra numbers being shipped should have signaled to the drug companies that people were taking too many pills.

The lawsuit argued that the wholesalers should have asked why the pharmacies ordered so many pills and reported the excessive drug orders to authorities. Instead of doing so, they earned money from the extra drug sales.

DEADLY DRUGS

The number of drug overdose deaths in the United States and some Canadian provinces has more than doubled in the past 10 years. The drugs connected to the most overdose deaths in southern West Virginia are hydrocodone and oxycodone. They are in a class of drugs called opioids. Deadly drugs such as heroin, fentanyl, and morphine, are also opioids.

These drugs act on the **nervous system** to relieve pain. They can also produce a "high" or a sense of pleasure and relaxation. Long-term use can lead to addiction. As addictions progress, addicts need to take higher and higher doses to experience the same effects. Hydrocodone and oxycodone abuse can lead to muscle spasms, severe vomiting, difficulty breathing, and heart failure.

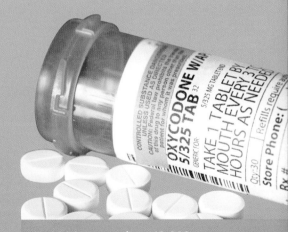

In 2016, more than 42,000 people died from opioid overdoses in the United States. In Canada, that number was more than 2,800.

A TEAM EFFORT

For five months after he received the sealed documents, Eric found time to examine the paperwork after his daily work was done.

What he read led him to ask more questions. He went back to court to ask that documents from other drug-related court cases be unsealed. He submitted a request under the **Freedom of Information Act** to access data from the Drug Enforcement Agency (DEA). This is the government agency that leads the country's efforts to stop the illegal selling and buying of drugs.

Eric also requested and received documents from the state health statistics center, which collects and stores health care information; the state pharmacy board, which licenses pharmacies and ensures they follow the laws; and the U.S. Centers for Disease Control and Prevention (CDC).

A team of people puts most large investigative journalism projects together. As his investigation progressed, Eric asked others to help him. He worked with lawyers to gain access to documents he needed. To review the paperwork, he worked side-by-side with a newsroom colleague, **data analyst** Andrew Brown.

Eric and Andrew spent months reviewing data and documents, **cross-checking** references, creating files, and analyzing numbers. They put the data together in ways that would help readers understand it. For example, the newspaper published maps that showed the number of painkiller dosages and overdoses in counties in West Virginia.

These tasks may sound boring. But it's this kind of painstaking—and crucial—detective work that fills in all the blanks a reporter needs before presenting a story to the public. For all the exciting public attention that an investigative journalism story might get, there are months, and even years, of unglamorous, behind-the-scenes work.

The Centers for Disease Control and Prevention (CDC) is a national organization that promotes good health, works to prevent illness, and researches health care issues.

ACCESSING INFORMATION

Most countries have Freedom of Information, or FOI, laws. These are designed to prevent governments from keeping secrets from their citizens. Any citizen, including a journalist, can request access to government documents under these laws. These might be such things as legal documents, police records, or financial statements. Under FOI laws, people can also access video and audio recordings, e-mails, maps, and photographs. Sometimes, journalists and other citizens request documents, but their requests are denied. This could be because the requested documents simply don't exist. There are also certain situations in which governments don't have to hand over information. For example, they can refuse to release information that could threaten national security, break laws, or invade a person's privacy.

*Since investigative journalism projects are long-lasting and have many moving parts, journalists need to collaborate with other professions, such as data analysts and **graphic designers**.*

PUTTING A NUMBER TO THE PROBLEM

Investigative journalists need data, or facts, statistics, and other information, to prove that their stories are true. Data can also help journalists fill in details in their stories and connect gaps. It's no surprise that data analysts are often important members of investigative journalism teams. They are professionals who review numbers to find trends and patterns. They also track, sort, and monitor digital, or online, information. Eric needed the help of data analyst Andrew Brown to make sense of the numbers and information found on the pages and pages of unsealed documents he received. With his help, Eric could finally make connections between the number of drug shipments and overdose deaths. "For the first time, we put a number to the problem," said Eric.

PUBLICATION

After reviewing the paperwork, Eric tracked down people who had been affected by the overdose crisis. He interviewed many of them, to include their stories in his investigative project. After months of reading, researching, and interviewing people, Eric finally had enough solid information to pull together his two-part series.

What he found—and reported in the *Charleston Gazette-Mail* newspaper and its online site—was this:

• During the period from 2007 to 2012, a number of major American drug wholesalers flooded small towns in southern West Virginia with hundreds of millions of prescription painkillers—specifically hydrocodone and oxycodone. They earned billions of dollars from these sales.

• During the same time frame, more than 1,700 individuals died from overdosing on these types of drugs, making West Virginia the overdose death capital of the country.

• The law requires that drug companies report "suspicious orders for controlled substances" from pharmacies.

That means they must report unusually large or unusually frequent orders. The drug companies did not file such reports. This led to the state's 2012 lawsuit against the drug companies—the one whose files were sealed, the one that started Eric's investigation. Since the lawsuit was filed in 2012, drug wholesalers have submitted thousands of suspicious reports.

• Eric counted 7,200 suspicious reports sitting, unopened, in cardboard boxes in 2016. The pharmacy board had not investigated a single one. Nor had it passed any of these reports to the DEA.

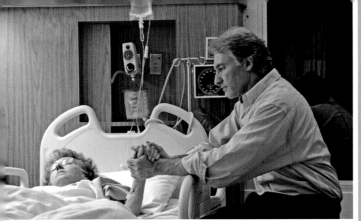

A PERSONAL CONNECTION

Personal stories are often an important part of investigative journalism projects. They can help readers see the perspective of people who are experiencing an issue. They illustrate the data in real life.

Eric's story connects the facts and statistics found in the documents with the story of a family grieving the overdose death of a loved one who was addicted to painkillers. The personal story and the data work together to create a well-rounded story. The story shows readers a real example of how the problem is affecting people. The data shows that the story is one of many—and proves that the story is part of a bigger problem.

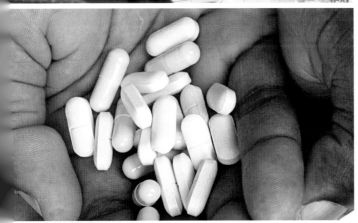

CHANGE-MAKING JOURNALISM

Eric Eyre's two-part series, "Painkiller Profiteers," was published in the *Charleston Gazette-Mail* in December 2016. After the story was made public, national newspapers, television networks, and online news sites interviewed Eric and conducted their own investigations into prescription drug abuse. His stories raised awareness of the issue across the country.

The project won the 2016 Pulitzer Prize for investigative journalism the following spring. It also won first place for investigative reporting in the Association for Health Care Journalists' 2016 Awards for Excellence, and a 2016 Scripps Howard Award for excellence in journalism.

> Reporter Eric Eyre showed how drug wholesalers routinely shipped vast quantities of pills to small, independent pharmacies and how West Virginia's Board of Pharmacy failed to enforce regulations that could have limited those sales. His findings were so clear and compelling that various agencies, including the Board of Pharmacy, had to take action.

Judge's comments, Association for Health Care Journalists Award for Excellence, 2017

The Association of Health Care Journalists is an organization that works to advance health care journalism in the public. It awards outstanding work in this specialized field of reporting each year.

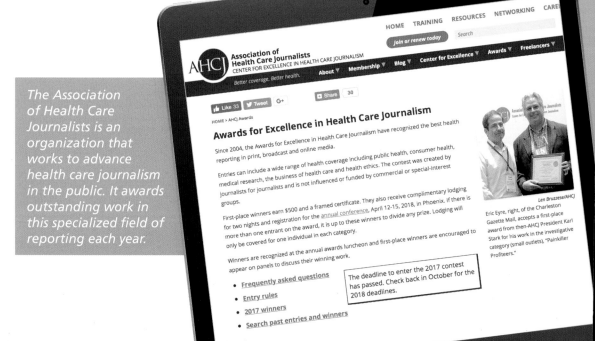

Association of Health Care Journalists
CENTER FOR EXCELLENCE IN HEALTH CARE JOURNALISM
Better coverage. Better health.

HOME   TRAINING   RESOURCES   NETWORKING   CAREE

Join or renew today   Search

About ▼   Membership ▼   Blog ▼   Center for Excellence ▼   Awards ▼   Freelancers ▼

Like 33   Tweet   G+   Share 30

HOME > AHCJ Awards

Awards for Excellence in Health Care Journalism

Since 2004, the Awards for Excellence in Health Care Journalism have recognized the best health reporting in print, broadcast and online media.

Entries can include a wide range of health coverage including public health, consumer health, medical research, the business of health care and health ethics. The contest was created by journalists for journalists and is not influenced or funded by commercial or special-interest groups.

First-place winners earn $500 and a framed certificate. They also receive complimentary lodging for two nights and registration for the annual conference, April 12-15, 2018, in Phoenix. If there is more than one entrant on the award, it is up to these winners to divide any prize. Lodging will only be covered for one individual in each category.

Winners are recognized at the annual awards luncheon and first-place winners are encouraged to appear on panels to discuss their winning work.

The deadline to enter the 2017 contest has passed. Check back in October for the 2018 deadlines.

- Frequently asked questions
- Entry rules
- 2017 winners
- Search past entries and winners

Len Bruzzese/AHCJ

Eric Eyre, right, of the Charleston Gazette Mail, accepts a first-place award from then-AHCJ President Karl Stark for his work in the investigative category (small outlets), "Painkiller Profiteers."

Career development
Freelance Center

Advocacy
Right-to-know
AHCJ actions

More importantly, Eric's series led to immediate changes in the prescription drug industry in West Virginia. The state pharmacy board quickly changed its ways. It now enforces the rule that drug companies must submit reports of suspicious orders. This has been law since 2001, but it had been ignored until Eric investigated and wrote about the problem. Now, as a result of Eric's work, the pharmacy board forwards suspicious pill orders to the DEA for investigation.

Since Eric's stories appeared in the newspaper, eight counties, at least 35 cities, and one town in West Virginia, have sued drug wholesalers. According to one lawyer involved in the case, the people suing the companies want to be paid for the problems they faced because of the drugs being oversold. For example, counties want the drug wholesalers to pay for the costs of sending people to **rehabilitation** facilities, where they are treated for addiction. The lawsuits are still in process, although the drug companies have recently paid West Virginia more than $36 million to settle the original (2012) lawsuits.

Eric continues to report on the progress of these lawsuits for the *Charleston Gazette-Mail*. In the first six months of 2018, he wrote more than 40 stories about the ongoing lawsuits and the continuing overdose crisis. He also remains a state reporter with daily deadlines.

"AT DEATH'S DOOR"

WHO	Hospice home-care providers
WHAT	Neglected dying patients
WHEN	2012–2017
WHERE	Across the United States
WHY	Lack of regulation and management
HOW	Care workers not showing up as scheduled, ignoring calls for help

Health and medical journalists around the world produce stories about the right to a healthy life and the need for quality health care. They may be print, broadcast, or online reporters, but their goals are the same—to raise awareness about health care issues, to question rules and laws related to health care, and to uncover medical systems that aren't working properly.

Hospices provide end-of-life care, which helps people spend their final days as peacefully as possible.

In 2017, a pair of American investigative health journalists, JoNel Aleccia and Melissa Bailey, got a tip about a health care system failing its patients. Hints from others, called tips, are often starting points for investigative journalism projects.

JoNel and Melissa work for Kaiser Health News. This a news service that reports on health care issues across the United States. One day, their editor told them about a horrible situation her friends had recently experienced. It involved hospice care—or, more correctly, a lack of hospice care.

Hospices provide end-of-life pain management and comfort. Sometimes this care takes place in facilities, similar to hospitals. Often, hospices offer home care, so individuals can spend their final days in their homes, with family and loved ones by their sides. It was this home hospice care that had failed the editor's friends.

JoNel and Melissa were told a story about how the editor's friends had not received the care they had been promised by the hospice providers. Despite being assured that hospice workers would be on call 24/7, they had received "little or no instruction or help" from them. Instead, hospice staff had simply dropped off boxes of medicine and supplies, and left. Sometimes, they arrived long after they'd promised to be there. At other times, they didn't show up at all.

The editor's friends reported calling emergency lines in times of crisis—and having nobody pick up the phone to help. One family even had to figure out how to perform a delicate medical procedure because a hospice worker was nowhere to be found.

FOLLOWING THE STORY

Investigative reporters know they can't blindly believe all the story tips that come their way. They know, especially in life-and-death health care situations, people can be emotional. This might cause them to exaggerate, leave out parts of the story, or forget things.

In this case, though, JoNel and Melissa sensed the situation was worth investigating. The stories sparked a question in the reporters' minds: What happens when hospice workers do not show up? This question was the starting point for what would become a lengthy investigative journalism project.

JoNel and Melissa spent the next nine months researching, reviewing documents, and tracking down people who had suffered because they received poor hospice care.

Through this research, they found many stories like those of the editor's friends— stories about hospice workers not showing up, not answering phones, and delaying visits. This lack of care led to people dying in pain, and relatives struggling to help their loved ones without any medical support.

> I called the hospice, and I said, 'We're in trouble. I need help right away.' I waited and waited. They never called back.

Laure Fuerstenberg, whose husband died in pain, in her arms

HOSPICE SERVICES

Hospices in the United States and Canada are regulated by federal and state or provincial laws. Professional organizations and associations also oversee them. Hospices are required to provide the following minimum services:

- Around-the-clock care, as needed—24 hours a day, seven days a week, including holidays
- Doctor and nurse on call at all times
- Care for physical, emotional, social, and spiritual needs
- Assist family in caregiving activities
- Nursing and physician care, physical therapy, speech therapy, homemaking support, medication, and dietary counseling, as needed
- Comfort for the patient
- A plan detailing the services that will be provided, when, and by whom

DIGGING THROUGH DATA

Accessing public information is a common way for investigative journalists to begin their investigations. The data, or information, found in public documents is one way journalists find out if a problem is happening to a lot of people.

JoNel and Melissa started their research at the Centers for Medicare & Medicaid Services (CMS). Medicare provides health coverage to Americans aged 65 and over. Medicaid provides health coverage for low-income individuals and families. This coverage includes hospice care.

To access CMS data, the reporters submitted a request through the Freedom of Information Act. Their request was granted. JoNel and Melissa soon received 20,000 hospice inspection reports from more than 4,000 hospices across the nation. The reports covered a five-year period, from January 2012 to February 2017.

The first thing the journalists did was search through the reports for stories of unacceptable hospice care. They used keywords such as "agony," "horror," "neglect," and "missed visit" to scan thousands of pages. They wanted to know if other people had been treated as badly as the editor's friends. Unfortunately, the reporters found many similar stories.

We found hundreds of instances of families reporting that hospice workers didn't show up as scheduled, left dying patients for hours with no pain medication, or failed to answer repeated calls for help.

JoNel Aleccia and Melissa Bailey, 2017

Together, Medicare and Medicaid pay almost $16 billion for hospice care for about 1.4 million Americans every year.

THE HUMAN ELEMENT

It would make a journalist's life easy if one set of documents provided all the information he or she needed—but that almost never happens. Typically, part of the investigative journalist's job is to track down and review a variety of sources.

In this case, JoNel and Melissa wanted to interview some of the people mentioned in the reports. They wanted to know how family and friends felt about the poor treatment of their loved ones in hospice care. It's not always easy to find people who want to share their stories. In JoNel and Melissa's case, they had documents showing that hundreds of people had been affected by poor hospice care. But the reports didn't identify patients by name. That meant the pair of reporters had to come up with another way to find people to interview.

They noticed that many of the records included clues, such as death dates, that pointed to the identity of patients.

Like detectives, they followed those clues to find some of those people. They scoured newspaper **obituaries** and other public records. Through these sources, they found the names of several patients who had suffered poor hospice care before they died.

Next, the reporters set out to locate relatives of the **deceased**. Again, they turned to public records—such as telephone books—and online sources, such as social media sites. Despite hitting many dead ends, they found relatives willing to tell their stories. JoNel and Melissa described the reaction of one woman, who "burst into tears on the phone, saying she had given up hope that anyone would care."

The reporters said the stories they heard during the interview process were "horrifying."

JoNel and Melissa heard countless stories about family and friends helplessly watching their loved ones dying in pain, without support from hospice workers.

INVESTIGATING FURTHER

Two qualities good investigative journalists possess are dedication to finding answers and using ingenuity, or inventiveness, to do so.

After scanning thousands of documents, and interviewing relatives of hospice patients, JoNel and Melissa had answered their first question: What happens when hospice workers do not show up? They learned that many people spent their final days in pain, while their family desperately tried to contact the hospices for help. They heard stories of a nurse who turned her cell phone off and missed 16 calls for help, and about a hospice that changed records to cover up its lack of necessary care.

Now that the reporters had this first answer, they had another question: How often do hospices let down dying patients? To answer this, they went back to the CMS paperwork—but the records weren't organized in a way that provided an obvious answer. JoNel and Melissa called on their ingenuity and creativity,

and came up with a method to figure out how widespread hospice **negligence** was. Their solution was to focus on inspections that began with complaints filed by friends and families of patients. That narrowed down the number of files they needed to review—from 20,000 to 3,800. JoNel and Melissa each read 1,900 records.

Based on these public complaints, the reporters discovered that inspectors had found wrongdoing at hundreds of hospices across the nation. In about half those cases—418, to be exact— the hospices had been found guilty of wrongdoing specifically related to providing poor-quality home care. That meant about 10 percent of hospices across the country had neglected home care patients who needed them.

JoNel and Melissa also discovered that hospices were rarely punished for providing poor care. Of the thousands that had been investigated by CMS during a five-year period (2012–2017), only 17 were required to close down. Others agreed to retrain staff members. Some simply promised to do better in the future.

CHANGE-MAKING JOURNALISM

Every story has many sides to it. People have different points of view, or ways of seeing and experiencing things. Good journalists document all sides of every story they cover.

With that in mind, in their final hospice article, JoNel and Melissa pointed out that most people are happy with the end-of-life care they receive. One recent study showed that 80 percent of hospice users rated the care as nine or ten out of ten. Another study showed that 89 percent of people were "satisfied" with their hospice experiences.

JoNel and Melissa also contacted hospices with complaints against them. They wanted to hear their views on the story.

Just a few of the hospices agreed to talk to the reporters. Of the ones that did, some said they had made changes and educated staff because of the complaints. Others said they couldn't comment because of privacy concerns. Some said they had done nothing wrong.

[Poor quality hospice care] is like medical malpractice. It's relatively rare, but when it happens, it tarnishes the entire field. "

**Amy Tucci,
Hospice Foundation
of America, 2017**

Journalists have a responsibility to learn about and report on all perspectives, or sides, of a story. A story from only one perspective may not be a fair or thorough look at the events that took place.

28

HELP FOR THE DYING

Hospices began in the United Kingdom (UK) and came to the United States in 1974. At the time, they were run by religious and not-for-profit organizations. In 1982, Medicare started covering hospice costs for Americans.

Since then, many hospices have become money-making businesses. Sometimes, to increase their earnings, unethical hospices might cut corners. This occasionally leads to poor care. Because they're funded by the government, hospices get paid no matter how good—or bad—their service is.

In addition, until 2018, hospices were not required to be inspected regularly. That means they were not watched as closely as other health care institutions.

As of 2018, though, the rules have changed. Now, hospices must be inspected at least once every three years.

In most cases, hospices do excellent work, offering top-quality care to patients and their families.

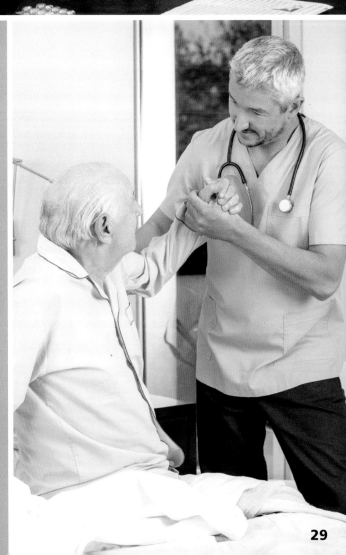

After nine months of reading reports, analyzing numbers, interviewing, and researching, JoNel Aleccia and Melissa Bailey published their findings on the Kaiser Health News website and in *Time* magazine.

Their story, titled "'No One Is Coming:' Hospice Patients Abandoned At Death's Door," was published in October 2017. It included text, photos, and video elements. It also included links to documents, regulations, articles, academic studies, and websites they used in their research.

Within a week, the story had been picked up, or republished, by *CNN*, *PBS Newshour*, the *Huffington Post*, and many other media outlets across the country.

Meanwhile, JoNel and Melissa were finalists for the National Institute for Health Care Management Foundation's 2017 Print Journalism Award. Both reporters continue to work on investigative projects for Kaiser Health News, focusing on aging and end-of-life health issues.

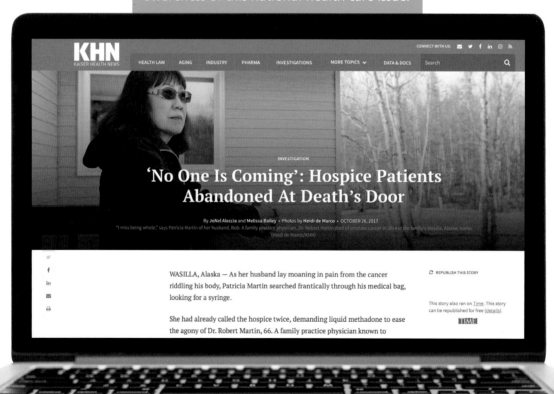

JoNel and Melissa's story has raised public awareness of this national health care issue.

VISUAL JOURNALISM

JoNel and Melissa's story included text, photos, and video elements. This is common in many investigative journalism projects today, because they are usually posted online.

Online investigative journalism projects are usually multimedia, meaning the stories are told using a variety of media. This includes text, photos, and videos, but also includes a wide range of visual elements—such as maps, charts, infographics, and more.

Different visual elements draw different viewers and readers, so the more variety there is in the presentation of a story, the more viewers it's likely to draw.

For this reason, media outlets usually send photographers and videographers with their reporters. Photographers take pictures to add faces, places, and visual details to a printed story. Videographers accompany reporters to record interviews and other footage related to a story. Most newsrooms have graphic artists who add other visual elements to a project.

Photojournalism uses a series of related photographs to tell a story. The viewer sees the story through pictures, with a small amount of text to read.

Video journalism projects tell stories through video. The story is told from one video journalist's perspective. The video journalist does it all—produces, reports, films, and edits the story.

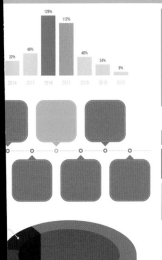

Infographics are images that use visuals, such as pictures and graphs, to clearly show data.

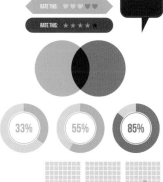

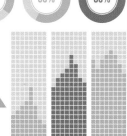

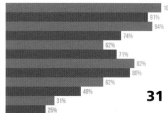

"UNSAFE AT ANY LEVEL"

WHO	Millions of American children
WHAT	Not tested for lead poisoning, as required by health officials
WHEN	2005–2015
WHERE	Across the United States
WHY	Inconsistent testing rules, differences between federal and state laws, rules ignored

Often, investigative journalists get their story ideas after hearing other news reports. They read or hear things that prompt them to ask further questions. That's how New York-based reporters Joshua Schneyer and Michael Pell came up with their award-winning collection of stories about lead poisoning. Each story they wrote led to another story, until they had produced a series of four in a one-year period.

It was a national news story about contaminated water in Flint, Michigan, that first inspired their investigation. In April 2014, the city of Flint changed its water source. It had been getting its tap water from the Detroit River and Lake Huron, but that had become too expensive. To save money, the city began pumping water from the Flint River into residents' homes.

Immediately, many residents became ill. Scientists soon discovered the water was contaminated with lead, a metal that causes serious damage to humans when ingested, or consumed.

For almost two years, the city received complaints from the public about the water—but officials insisted there was nothing wrong with it.

Some citizens launched legal action. Scientists conducted more tests and studies to prove the water was contaminated. Finally, in December 2015, city politicians admitted the water was tainted. They agreed to switch back to the original water source.

*The city of Flint, and Genessee **county** where it is located, declared a **state of emergency**.*

DANGER **LEAD HAZARD** WORK AREA KEEP OUT
NO SMOKING, EATING, OR DRINKING

CHEMICAL CONTENT

Lead is a heavy metal that is found in Earth's crust. Everyone has a tiny bit of lead in his or her body at birth. Too much lead in the body can lead to a variety of health problems.

Lead poisoning can cause stomach pains, vomiting, headaches, organ damage, high blood pressure, and seizures. In children, it can cause brain damage that leads to learning disabilities, developmental delays, and other lifelong mental health issues.

In the past, many household products contained lead, including paint, pipes and other plumbing materials, floor tiles, and pottery. Lead was banned from paint in 1978. Lead in other products—including gasoline for cars—was banned in the 1980s. Houses older than 1978, though, probably still have lead paint on the walls.

A blood test for lead takes about three minutes. The costs of children's lead blood tests are covered by health care programs in the United States and Canada.

FOR USE AS A MOTOR FUEL ONLY
CONTAINS LEAD
(TETRAETHYL)

A WIDESPREAD PROBLEM

This national news story sparked reporters Joshua Schneyer and Michael Pell to start asking questions about lead poisoning. "It made us wonder: If Flint's problem could go undiscovered for months... where else was lead poisoning happening?" said Joshua.

The reporters, who worked for Reuters news service, decided to investigate. They first looked at other water sources around the country—including well water. They read university studies and government reports that revealed that well water often contained unacceptably high levels of lead. That meant millions of Americans had been drinking, bathing in, and cooking with lead-contaminated water.

After they found this serious problem, Joshua and Michael interviewed families affected by tainted water. Through these interviews, they learned that most American children are not tested for lead in their bloodstreams—even though many laws and regulations state that they should be. They also learned that the blood of many children who used well water contained higher lead levels than the kids in Flint.

In March 2016, Joshua and Michael published their findings in a story about lead poisoning in well water on the Reuters website. It was titled "A Quest for Clean Water."

Investigative journalism projects typically answer important questions. Sometimes, though, they raise further questions in reporters' minds. This was the case for Joshua and Michael and their lead poisoning investigation.

While preparing the well water story, they wanted to know why most American children had not had lead blood tests and how this lack of testing affected kids. They launched a second lead-related investigation.

NEWS OF THE WORLD

Joshua Schneyer and Michael Pell work for Reuters, an international news agency based in London, UK. Reuters publishes stories, videos, and photos on its website. It also distributes those stories to news outlets around the world. More than 3,000 journalists, photographers, and videographers work for Reuters in 200 locations around the world.

Reuters is the second largest of more than 100 major news agencies around the globe. It was founded in 1851. The largest, founded in 1846, is New York City-based Associated Press (AP). Founded in 1835, the oldest news agency in the world—and third largest—is Agence France-Presse.

All three of these news agencies, and many others, have teams of journalists specializing in investigative reporting.

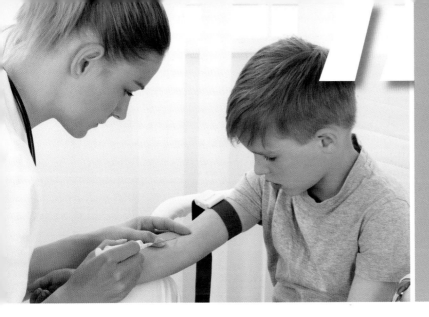

> Millions of children are falling through the cracks of early childhood lead testing requirements.

Joshua Schneyer and Michael Pell, Reuters, 2016

REVIEWING THE DATA

Like many investigative journalists, they started their research with public documents. They requested and reviewed children's blood test records from state health departments, Medicaid, and the Centers for Disease Control and Prevention (CDC).

Children enrolled in Medicaid are required to receive two blood tests for lead before age three. Several states require the same thing. The CDC recommends that all children be tested. If high lead levels are detected early, the kids can be treated.

The documents Joshua and Michael read showed that only 11 states required early lead testing—and in those states, fewer than half the children were tested. Nationwide, as few as five percent of Medicaid children were tested as required.

In Flint, Michigan, where the water crisis had attracted national attention, about five percent of kids had high lead levels. Joshua and Michael found many states where at least twice that number of kids had far more lead in their blood than the Flint kids did.

Investigative journalists must fully understand a topic before they present it to the public. They have to make sure all their facts are correct, and all the relevant questions are answered. To accomplish this, Joshua and Michael interviewed dozens of health experts. To add a human element to their story, they also talked to family members of 15 children who suffered from lead poisoning.

After three months of researching, analyzing numbers, and interviewing, Joshua and Michael published their second story about lead poisoning. "Unsafe at Any Level" appeared on the Reuters website in June 2016. But these investigative reporters weren't finished with this subject just yet.

THE INVESTIGATION CONTINUES

As they dug deeper and deeper into the subject of lead testing in American children for their first two stories, Joshua and Michael found one particularly disturbing situation. They heard about a public housing complex in Indiana that was being demolished because of toxic lead levels in the soil.

In 2016, all 1,100 residents had to move out of the housing complex because the soil contained three times the acceptable amount of lead.

Shockingly, five years earlier, a branch of the CDC made a statement that said the neighborhood was completely safe. It reported almost all children in the area had blood tests, and those tests showed low lead levels.

Clearly the area was not safe. Joshua and Michael wanted to know how such an error could happen. They decided to investigate the CDC's statement.

That's when they learned that the data used by the CDC in their statement was incomplete. Lead test results are tracked by state and by smaller, community areas. Statewide numbers might show that just a few kids in an entire state have too much lead in their blood. But these numbers don't show where in the state those kids live. All of the affected kids could be in one neighborhood. Smaller community test results are needed to learn where the affected kids live. State results alone do not show this information.

That's what happened in the case of this particular Indiana neighborhood. The CDC had not looked at neighborhood-level data when it declared the community safe from lead poisoning. The CDC had put hundreds of children at risk because their safety statement had been based on incomplete information.

In September 2016, Joshua and Michael wrote the third story in their lead-poisoning series. This one, called "Toxins in the Soil," focused on the situation in the Indiana neighborhood.

DO NOT
PLAY IN THE DIRT OR
AROUND THE MULCH

⊕EPA

The homes in the West Calamut housing complex in Indiana had been built in the early 1970s on the site of a company that made lead paint. Nearby were two other factories that produced lead-based products. Signs there warned children not to play in the dirt.

Some of the contamination here [in this Indiana neighborhood] is at higher levels than we would consider hazardous waste.

Michael Breakoff, Environmental Protection Agency (EPA), 2012

37

SEARCHING FOR NUMBERS

Now that the reporters knew neighborhood blood test results were available, they launched another, related, investigation.

This time, they wanted to view blood test results at the community level. They wanted to pinpoint pockets of lead poisoning. The problem was, this data had rarely been made public.

Joshua and Michael sent records requests to health departments in all 50 states, and to the CDC. In some cases, they had to submit requests under the Freedom of Information Act to get the numbers they wanted. Some states couldn't send data because they didn't have it. Others didn't respond to the reporters' requests, or wanted to charge them money for the information. Some officials said privacy laws prevented them from sharing the numbers.

In the end, Joshua and Michael received data from 34 states. It was the first time anyone had ever studied these numbers.

Journalists often struggle to get data from governments and other official institutions. That was the case for Joshua and Michael as they continued their investigation.

The scope of the lead problem went way beyond what we could have imagined. Nearly 3,000 neighborhoods...had rates of elevated childhood blood tests at least twice as high as Flint's.

Joshua Schneyer, 2017

Often, investigative journalists uncover stories that aren't deliberately kept secret, but are so buried in paperwork that nobody has taken the time to dig through it. Reporters discover such data exists only because someone happens to mention it during their research. That's what happened in this case.

As the numbers "trickled in," Joshua and Michael built a database to track them. They came up with a system to deal with missing data and differences between states. They consulted data analysts to confirm that their process made sense.

The numbers revealed that millions of children across the country were not being tested for lead poisoning as required. The reporters also found almost 3,000 neighborhoods with lead poisoning rates at least double those of Flint, Michigan.

Even more frightening, said Joshua, was that this data only represented 60 percent of the American population. "There are many more poisoned neighborhoods left uncharted."

As their investigation required them to make sense of numbers and patterns, Joshua and Michael needed to check with data analysts to make sure that their conclusions were accurate.

CHANGE-MAKING JOURNALISM

Joshua and Michael spent months gathering and analyzing data—but this was just the beginning. "The biggest challenge" (in this investigation) said Joshua, "was to show readers the human side of a depressing story—one in which our subjects, poisoned children, will grow up with stark disadvantages."

The data they had didn't name names. They had to figure out a way to find kids affected by lead poisoning. They "crisscrossed the country" looking for people affected by lead poisoning. They visited neighborhoods in high-risk areas. They talked to local officials. They knocked on doors, and approached families whose children were playing outside. They asked to speak to them about their experiences with lead poisoning.

Investigative journalists might find a lot of information in documents, studies, and government reports—but it's important that they also travel to places affected by the story in question. That's where they see the true impact of a situation. In this case, the reporters found many people who had no idea their children were at risk.

In December 2016, Joshua Schneyer and Michael Pell published their findings in the fourth installment of their lead-poisoning series, "Off the Charts." It featured an interactive map that showed lead levels in thousands of zip codes across the country. This map has been viewed by thousands of people. For the first time, this map allowed people to see whether children in their specific neighborhoods were at risk for lead poisoning.

Not only did the lead stories raise public awareness, but they also led to immediate change.

REUTERS INVESTIGATES

Exposing the hidden hazards of lead poisoning across America

Unsafe at Any Level

A REUTERS SERIES

LEAD FEARS: Krystle Jackson moved her family out of a housing complex in Indiana after two of her children tested high for lead. Here, Kavon, 1, and Kaydance, 3, sleep in REUTERS/Michelle Kanaar

Off the Charts

A Reuters analysis of blood lead-test results across the thousands of communities with poisoning rates above Flint, Michigan. FULL STORY

Unsafe at Any Level

It isn't just Flint: Many states and Medicaid rules requ for young children, but millions are falling through th FULL STORY

A Quest for Clean Water

Millions of Americans who rely on private wells for may be ingesting dangerous levels of lead, Reuters re academic research shows. FULL STORY

Toxins in the Soil

Reuters finds flawed CDC report left Indiana children lead poisoning. FULL STORY

The story was immediately broadcast by major media outlets, including CBS News, Fox News, and PBS Newshour. Dozens of bloggers and smaller media outlets also wrote stories on the subject.

As soon as the final story in Joshua and Michael's series was published, local governments, health officials, and researchers across the country demanded change. They pushed for more blood screening for children, for community outreach programs that would educate the public about lead poisoning, more tests for lead content in buildings and soil, and more funding to pay for these initiatives.

Federal government officials also pushed for increased testing, and Medicaid acknowledged the flaws in its testing process. Scientists and researchers used the reporters' data to launch further studies.

The reporters also received great recognition from their peers. They won awards from the Columbia School of Journalism and the National Press Club, and a Sidney Award for "outstanding socially conscious journalism."

Today, Joshua and Michael continue to work on investigative projects for Reuters. They also continue to update their lead-testing data. A year after the final story in their series was made public, they published another article with new numbers. As of January 2017, Michael and Joshua had counted almost 4,000 American communities in 34 states with childhood lead-poisoning rates at least double those in Flint, Michigan, at the time of its water crisis.

Scientists take samples of soil to test it in a lab for any unsafe materials, such as lead.

" The winners used unpublished data to expose a nationwide public health threat. Some local officials didn't even know about their lead problem until Reuters crunched the numbers. "

Lindsay Beyerstein, Sidney Award judge, 2017

CONCLUSION

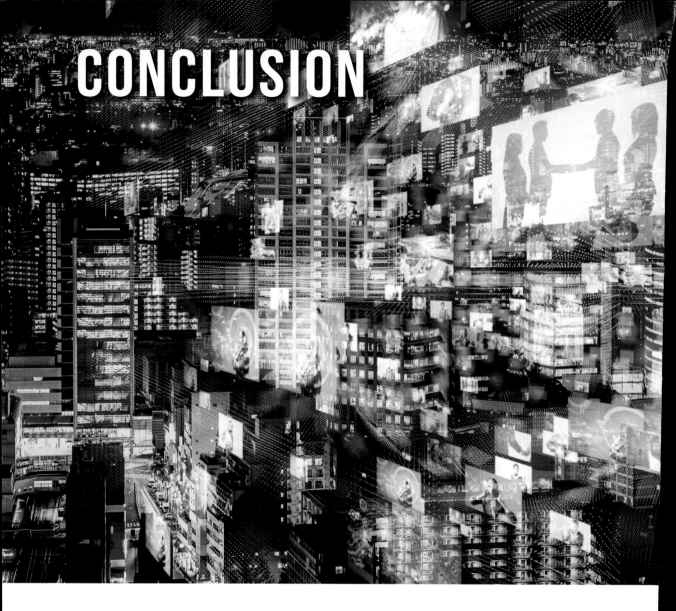

Whether they research issues related to health care, the environment, human rights, or other topics, investigative journalists dig deep. They tackle subjects that other journalists don't cover. These are often topics that have been hidden from the public view—either on purpose or because the subject matter is so complicated that nobody's ever looked deeply enough.

Sometimes investigative journalists, such as JoNel Aleccia and Melissa Bailey who wrote the hospice story, ask questions that others have never asked. They give voice to people who are voiceless and suffering. They uncover stories the world doesn't know about. Their work informs the public about important national and international concerns. They expose wrongdoing, bad behavior, and abuse of power.

In a time when our inboxes and social media streams are flooded with videos, texts, photos, and news stories—some real, some fake—investigative journalists can help us make informed choices about the issues affecting our world.

Investigative journalists provide information so that citizens—like those affected by lead poisoning in the story by Joshua Schneyer and Michael Pell—can demand change, ask for help, or make informed choices about the things that affect their lives.

Even in today's fast-paced world, investigative journalists take the time to get things right. They often spend months or years studying a particular subject. Like Eric Eyre in his research for the prescription drug overdose story, they review data and documents. They check and double-check their facts. They interview a lot of people.

Investigative journalists are curious, independent, determined reporters whose goal is to find and expose the truth for the benefit of their communities and the world.

BIBLIOGRAPHY

CHAPTER 1

"Investigative Journalism." UNESCO, n.d. https://bit.ly/1fhnmej

Kemp, Kenny. "Gazette-Mail wins Pulitzer for investigative reporting." *Charleston Gazette-Mail*, April 10, 2017. https://bit.ly/2woVTDK

"Mission & Goals." Association of Health Care Journalists, 2018. https://bit.ly/2wyamxv

"Mission." Association of Health Care Journalists, 2018. https://healthjournalism. org/center-mission.php

"Statement of Principles of the Association of Health Care Journalists." Association of Health Care Journalists, 2018. https://healthjournalism.org/ secondarypage-details.php?id=56

University of Charleston Speaker Series: Eric Eyre. 2017. https://bit.ly/2BYEPdZ

CHAPTER 2

Asbury, Kayla. "Hearings in WV drug wholesale lawsuits begin." *Charleston Gazette-Mail*, June 20, 2017. https://bit.ly/2LAAZqQ

Eyre, Eric. "Drug firms fueled 'pill mills' in rural WV." *Charleston Gazette-Mail*, May 23, 2016. https://bit.ly/2LtQuRz

Eyre, Eric. "Drug firms poured 780M painkillers into WV amid rise of overdoses." *Charleston Gazette-Mail*, December 17, 2016. https://bit.ly/2DO0xP3

Eyre, Eric. "Probing court records helps uncover West Virginia opioid profits." Association of Health Care Journalists, May 5, 2017. https://bit.ly/2wuEkCv

Gupta, Arka. "On the Opioid Epidemic, Part 1: An Interview with Pulitzer Prize-Winner Eric Eyre." *The Politic*, June 12, 2017. https://bit.ly/2wlajG0

Kounang, Nadia. "Opioids now kill more people than breast cancer." CNN, December 21, 2017. https://cnn.it/2BTbtMH

"Prescription Opioids." Canadian Centre on Substance Abuse and Addiction. September 2017. https://bit.ly/2Np99mk

CHAPTER 3

Aleccia, JoNel, and Melissa Bailey. "'No One Is Coming': Hospice Patients Abandoned At Death's Door." Kaiser Health News, October 26, 2017. https://bit.ly/2olw4kA

Aleccia, JoNel, and Melissa Bailey. "Reporters' data analysis added credibility to anecdotal evidence of hospice neglect." Association of Health Care Journalists, December 20, 2017. https://bit.ly/2Nx49ZJ

CHAPTER 4

Beyerstein, Lindsay. "Worse Than Flint: Reuters Wins January Sidney for Exposing a National Epidemic of Lead Poisoning." The Sidney Hillman Foundation, January 2017. https://bit.ly/2jiPfl8

Schneyer, Joshua, and M.B. Pell. "Flawed CDC report left Indiana children vulnerable to lead poisoning." *Reuters Investigates*, September 28, 2016. https://reut.rs/2PdreRQ

Schneyer, Joshua, and M.B. Pell. "Millions of American children missing early lead tests, Reuters finds." *Reuters Investigates*, June 9, 2016. www.reuters.com/investigates/special-report/lead-poisoning-testing-gaps

FURTHER READING

BOOKS

Bodden, Valerie. *Prescription and Over-the-Counter Drugs* (Drugs in Real Life), Essential Library, 2018.

Fromowitz, Lori. *12 Great Moments That Changed Newspaper History* (Great Moments in Media), 12-Story Library, 2015.

Mahoney, Ellen. *Nellie Bly and Investigative Journalism for Kids: Mighty Muckrakers from the Golden Age to Today*, Chicago Review Press, Inc., 2015.

WEBSITES

This page on the National Institute on Drug Abuse for Teens provides teenagers with everything they need to know about prescription painkillers. It also has links to videos, infographics, articles, and a blog.
https://teens.drugabuse.gov/drug-facts/prescription-pain-medications-opioids

This page on the *BBC*'s education website answers questions about the media industry in general, and each specific type of media. It includes videos, infographics, and quizzes to test readers' knowledge.
www.bbc.com/education/guides/zqrdxsg/revision/1

The Investigative Journalism Manual website provides everything you need to know about the field of investigative journalism.
www.investigative-manual.org/en

LINKS TO ARTICLES IN THIS BOOK

Chapters 1–2

Eyre, Eric. "Drug firms poured 780M painkillers into WV amid rise of overdoses." *Charleston Gazette-Mail*, December 17, 2016.
https://bit.ly/2DO0xP3

Eyre, Eric. "'Suspicious' drug order rules never enforced by state." *Charleston Gazette-Mail*, December 18, 2016.
https://bit.ly/2PcKSNG

Chapter 3

Aleccia, JoNel, and Melissa Bailey. "'No One Is Coming': Hospice Patients Abandoned At Death's Door." *Kaiser Health News*, October 26, 2017.
https://bit.ly/2olw4kA

Chapter 4

Schneyer, Joshua, and M.B. Pell. "Unsafe at Any Level." *Reuters Investigates*, 2016.
www.reuters.com/investigates/section/usa-lead

GLOSSARY

accountable To be made to take responsibility for one's actions

activists People who take action to support a cause

addiction Physical and/or emotional dependence on a substance

Attorney General The head legal officer who represents a country or state

chaotic Confused, disordered, messy, out of control

chronic Long lasting; persistent

concealed Hidden

confirm To prove that something is true or correct

copyright Laws that give a person the right to reproduce and distribute work, such as music or writing

county A region that has its own local government

court A place where legal matters are debated and decided

cross-checking Confirming something by using various sources

data analyst Someone who collects and analyzes data, and uses it to solve a problem

deceased Dead

doses The quantities or amounts of something, usually a medicine, that are prescribed

drug A medicine or other substance that has an effect on the body

editor A person at a newspaper who chooses stories to be featured and ensures stories have no factual, spelling, or grammatical errors

ethics Ideas about right and wrong behavior

Freedom of Information Act A law that prevents governments from keeping secrets from its citizens

graphic designer Someone who assembles texts and graphics to create design in ads, books, or magazines

harassing Repeatedly bothering or attacking someone

HIV/AIDS An illness that reduces the body's ability to fight infection and disease

instinct A person's natural ability or tendency to act a certain way

integrity Honesty, honor, ethical principles, high moral standards

lawsuit A legal claim or dispute that is settled in court by a judge

legal Related to law

malaria A potentially deadly disease that results in fever, chills, and sweating

mild Not strong or powerful

negligence Failure to give appropriate care and attention to someone or something

nervous system The part of the body that includes the brain, spinal cord, and nerves, and transmits messages to and from the brain and other parts of the body

obituaries Notices informing the public that someone has died

overdose death rate A number that compares the number of deaths by overdose with the population of an area

overdoses Deaths caused by taking too much of a particular prescription medication, illegal drug, or alcohol

painstaking Describing actions done with extreme care and attention to detail

pharmaceutical Relating to medicine or drugs

pharmacists People who are trained to dispense, or distribute, medications

policies A plan of action or set of guidelines usually created and followed by a government or organization

polio A disease that leads to muscle weakness, especially in the legs; it can lead to paralysis, even death

politics Activities associated with running a country, state, or town

proactive Taking action, rather than waiting for something to happen

profiteers People who make, or try to make, an overly large or unfair profit

profits Money that is made

Pulitzer Prize The highest award for journalism, literature, and music in the United States

racial inequalities When people are not given advantages, opportunities, or fair treatment because of their race

reform An action, plan, or rule that is meant to improve something

rehabilitation Treatment for addiction

sealed (court documents) To have had a procedure applied that prevents sensitive or confidential information from becoming public record

sources People, or documents, videos, recordings, or other publications, that provide information to a journalist

state of emergency A dangerous situation in which a government gives itself special powers to resolve the situation and protect citizens from danger

trade secrets Processes, techniques, recipes, or other business information that, if released to the public, would harm the business

United Nations An international organization made up of 193 countries that works to promote world peace and human rights

INDEX

ABOUT THE AUTHOR

Diane Dakers has been a print and broadcast journalist since 1991. She specializes in culture, science, and business reporting. She has also written 24 nonfiction and 3 fiction books for youth.